dick bruna

round, square, triangle

Tate Publishing

round

square

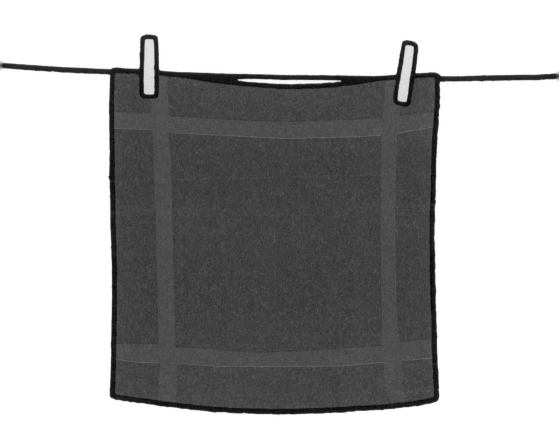

triangle

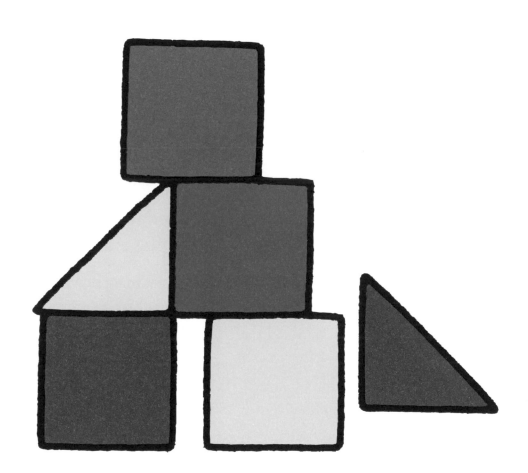

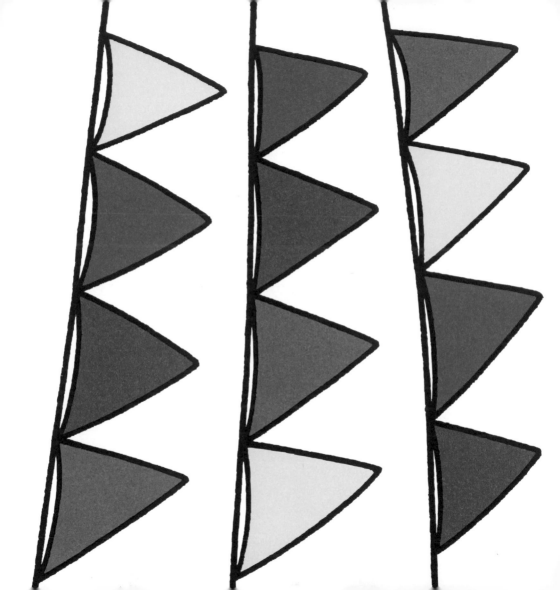

round
square
triangle

Other Dick Bruna books available from Tate Publishing:

I can count 2012
miffy the artist 2008
my vest is white 2012

Published 2012 by order of the Tate Trustees
by Tate Publishing, a division of Tate Enterprises Ltd,
Millbank, London SW1P 4RG
www.tate.org.uk/publishing

This edition © Tate 2012

Original edition: *rond, vierkant, driehoekig*
Original text Dick Bruna © copyright Mercis Publishing bv, 1982
Illustrations Dick Bruna © copyright Mercis Publishing bv, 1982
Publication licensed by Mercis Publishing bv, Amsterdam
Printed by Sachsendruck Plauen GmbH, Germany
All rights reserved.

A catalogue record for this book is available from the British Library
ISBN 978 1 84976 077 5
Distributed in the United States and Canada by ABRAMS, New York
Library of Congress Control Number: applied for

MIX

From responsible
sources

FSC® C021195